I CAN HELP
Save Energy

Viv Smith

W
FRANKLIN WATTS
LONDON • SYDNEY

First Published in 1998 by
Franklin Watts
This edition 2001

Franklin Watts
96 Leonard Street
London EC2A 4XD

© Franklin Watts 1998

Franklin Watts Australia
56 O'Riordan Street
Alexandria, Sydney
NSW 2015

Editor: Helen Lanz
Art Director: Robert Walster
Designer: Sally Boothroyd
Environmental consultant: John Baines
Commissioned photography: Steve Shott
Illustrations: Kim Woolley

Printed in Hong Kong

ISBN: 0 7496 4293 9
Dewey Decimal Number: 333.791
A CIP catalogue record for this book is
available from the British Library.

Picture Credits Cover: Steve Shott
Interior pictures: Commission for the New
Towns 20; Franklin Watts 6 (Steve Shott),
10, 12 (Ray Moller), 15 bl & tr, 27 tr & br
(Ray Moller); Owens-Corning Building
Products (UK) Ltd 16, 29; Robert Harding
Picture Library 13; Still Pictures 10 bl, 18, 22 t,
24 t. All other photographs by Steve Shott.

The publishers would like to thank St
Leonard's Primary School, Stafford, for their
help and enthusiasm, especially Viv Smith
and Class 2S who feature in this series.

Thank you also to Still Pictures for
photographs supplied for this book.

Contents

Energy for everything   6

From fuel to energy   8

Burning fuels   10

Using energy   12

Save it!   14

Wrap it up   16

Take a walk   18

Muscle power   20

Endless energy   22

Use with care   24

More activities and facts   26

Useful words   28

Index   30

Energy for everything

Feel the cold from a fridge, the warmth from a radiator or watch a washing machine spin. See a car go by or an aeroplane take off. All these things are using energy.

Energy is invisible, but it makes things move, stop, warm up or cool down, make sounds or give out light. Most energy comes from fuels such as coal, oil or gas.

Bikes, cars and buses need fuel to make them go.

Make a chart like this to help you find out about the different types of energy at home.

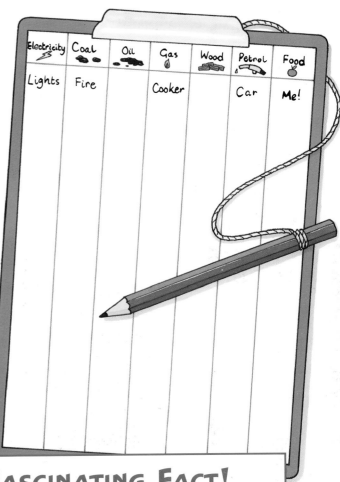

Electricity	Coal	Oil	Gas	Wood	Petrol	Food
Lights	Fire		Cooker		Car	Me!

FASCINATING FACT!

The earth's energy comes from the sun. The sun is a star. It is about 150 million kilometres away.

From fuel to energy

Coal, oil and gas release energy when they are burned. Nuclear energy is released when tiny pieces (called atoms) in special metals are split apart.

But where do these fuels that give us energy come from?

Plants which died millions of years ago that have rotted down and are dug out of the ground. = **coal**

Tiny animals which died millions of years ago and have been crushed together and are drilled out of rocks. = **oil and gas**

Special metals in rocks are dug from the ground. Atoms in the metal are split apart. This releases energy.

= **nuclear energy**

Plants and animals which are eaten by people and other animals to provide energy needed to keep warm, move and walk. = **food**

Coal, oil and gas take a very long time to form and once they are gone, we cannot replace them. Nuclear fuel creates a waste that is difficult to get rid of. We have to use fuel and the energy it gives us carefully.

Burning fuels

Burning fossil fuels for their energy causes problems.

Gases given off when these fuels are burned pollute the air. Some of these gases mix with water already in the air to make 'acid rain'. This can kill trees and plants when it falls. It can also damage buildings.

Another problem with burning fossil fuels is the 'greenhouse effect'. A greenhouse gets warm inside because heat from the sun is trapped by the glass and can only escape slowly. This is similar to what is happening to the earth.

The Greenhouse Effect

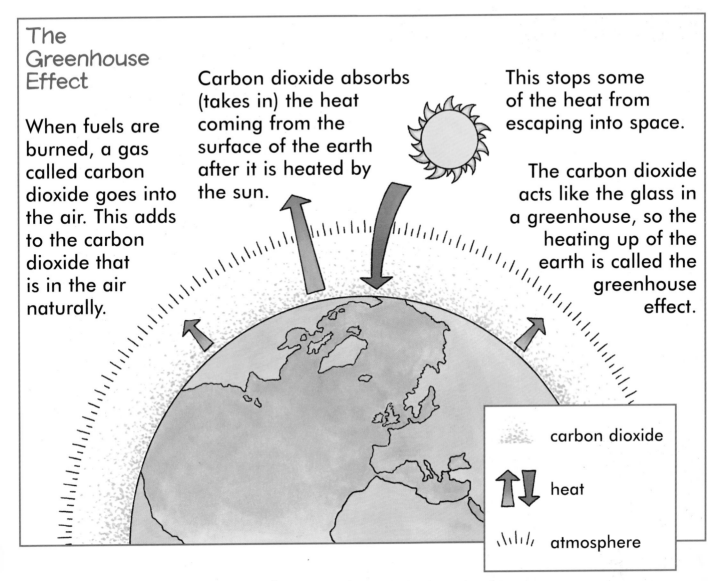

When fuels are burned, a gas called carbon dioxide goes into the air. This adds to the carbon dioxide that is in the air naturally.

Carbon dioxide absorbs (takes in) the heat coming from the surface of the earth after it is heated by the sun.

This stops some of the heat from escaping into space.

The carbon dioxide acts like the glass in a greenhouse, so the heating up of the earth is called the greenhouse effect.

carbon dioxide

heat

atmosphere

Not only do we have to be careful that we do not use too much fuel too quickly, we also need to try and use fuels that are cleaner and don't pollute the earth.

FASCINATING FACT!

The greenhouse effect is making the earth warmer. This is changing the weather around the world.

Using energy

Over a third of the energy in Britain is used by people in their homes.

Think about the times when you use the most electricity during the day. Is it when you get up? Perhaps it is when the main meal is being cooked? How much electricity is used when you are asleep?

 HAVE A GO!

Draw a picture to show the different kinds of electrical equipment you have at home. Where do they belong? Which room has the most equipment?

12

We use energy in different ways. Sometimes we just plug in the equipment we use and switch it on. Sometimes we want energy which we can move about, so we use a battery.

✳ WATCH OUT!

Electricity can be VERY dangerous. Never do anything with it unless you have adult help.

Be careful when you touch batteries. Ask an adult to put them in and take them out for you.

There are chemicals in a battery. When they mix, electrical energy is given out.

👀 LOOK BACK

Look at the picture you have drawn. How many things run on battery power? Which ones need plugging in?

❗ FASCINATING FACT!

Over 400 million batteries are used in Britain every year. Rechargeable batteries can be used many times over.

Save it!

If you were last person to leave a room at home or school today, did you leave the lights on and the door open? Does your radio play whether you are there to listen to it or not? Is your video recorder on standby all day?

If these things happen then you are wasting a lot of energy.

✂ HAVE A GO!

Find out which electrical things in your house are left on for the longest time. Design a 'Save It!' poster to remind everyone how they can help to save electricity.

Washing machines and tumble driers use a lot of energy to get your clothes clean and dry. You can help make sure they always have a full load when they are used.

On most days, the sun and wind will dry your washing.

FASCINATING FACT!

Energy-saving light bulbs use a quarter of the energy of an ordinary light bulb and last ten times as long.

Wrap it up

It is no good using energy to heat a house if most of the heat escapes through the walls, roof and windows.

Double-glazed windows and a thick layer of special material in the roof can help keep the warmth in and the cold out. This is called 'insulating' your house.

HAVE A GO!

How draughty are your windows? Hold a thin strip of tissue-paper near to them. Is it blown inwards by cold air coming in?

By having insulation in your loft, you can keep a lot of heat in your house.

FASCINATING FACT!

Some houses in Sweden are so well insulated that the heat given off by people's bodies is almost enough to keep the house warm, even in the coldest winter.

HAVE A GO!

To find out how insulation works, collect six empty drinks cans. Leave one uncovered but wrap the other five in different materials such as paper, cooking foil, thin fabric, cotton wool and woollen cloth.

Get an adult to pour the same amount of hot water into each can.

WATCH OUT!

Hot water can scald. Ask an adult to help you boil the kettle and fill the cans.

Which one stays the warmest for the longest time? Can you think why?

Take a walk

Cars, lorries, trains, aeroplanes and ships all use up a lot of energy. Most of them burn fuels which pollute the air.

If everyone walked or cycled when they went on short journeys, just think how much fuel would be saved and how much cleaner the air would be.

FASCINATING FACT!

In one year a car can produce over four times its own weight in carbon dioxide.

LOOK BACK

Look back to page 11 to find out how carbon dioxide pollutes our air.

HAVE A GO!

How do you get to school? Do a survey to find out how everyone in your class travels to school. Draw a bar-chart to show what you find out.

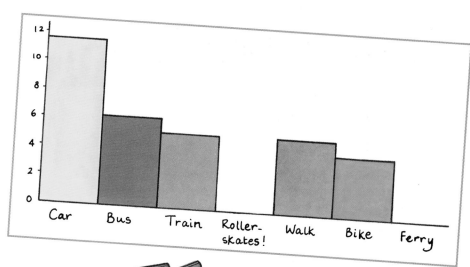

What does the chart tell you?

WATCH OUT!

Always make sure you are with an adult if you walk or cycle to school.

HAVE A GO!

It takes a lot of energy to make new things. We can help to save energy by re-using and recycling many of the things that we usually throw away.

Muscle power

Cycling and walking use muscle power only and do not pollute the air.

In many towns and cities people are encouraged to leave their cars at home or use them less often.

Here are some ways this can be done:

- ❁ Cycle-lanes and 'park-and-ride' schemes in towns.

- ❁ Electric trains or trams.

- ❁ Cheaper bus services that run more often.

Does your local town have any of these?

Towns that are built today usually have cycle lanes. The people who plan the new towns know that cycling is an important form of transport.

✂ HAVE A GO!

Plan short journeys from your home to school, the shops or to visit friends. Draw a map to help you. Can you walk, cycle or go by bus? What might help you decide which to choose?

- ❀ Do you live near a bus stop?
- ❀ What's the weather like?
- ❀ Do you have much to carry?

⬤ FASCINATING FACT!

More than a third of all the fuel used in Britain is used for transport.

Endless energy

Coal, gas and oil are energy sources that cannot be replaced. Sunlight and wind are natural sources of energy which can be used over and over again.

Energy that is created by the sun is called solar energy. Special panels collect the light and heat from the sun's rays and turn it into energy that we can use.

Can you see the panels where the light is collected on this calculator? What do you think would happen if you covered up these panels?

FASCINATING FACT!

Space-stations and satellites use solar panels to collect sunlight to turn it into electricity.

Fly a kite or run around on a windy day. Can you feel the power of the wind?

People have been using wind power for windmills and for sailing ships for hundreds of years.

FASCINATING FACT!

Modern windmills (like the one on page 22) are specially built to capture the power of the wind to make electricity.

HAVE A GO!

You can make a windmill out of a square of thin card, a pin, a bead and a stick. Ask an adult to help you.

1. Draw a cross on a square piece of card as shown in the first picture below. Mark the centre of the card.

2. Make a mark $\frac{3}{4}$ of the way down each line.

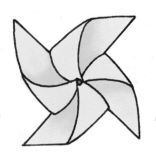

3. Cut down to each mark with a pair of scissors.

4. Pull alternate corners towards the centre.

5. Push the bead onto the pin. Push the pin through the card and into the stick.

Blow hard and watch it spin!

Use with care

Turn on a tap. Put your hand under the running water. Can you feel the force of the water?

Water is another natural source of energy that can be used again and again. It can be stored in huge lakes behind dams (above right). It is then allowed to flow through a pipe to turn wheels to make electricity. The tides of the sea can also be used to make electricity.

✂ HAVE A GO!

Ask an adult to help you make a water wheel from a flower pot, some plastic, a cork and 2 plastic knitting needles.

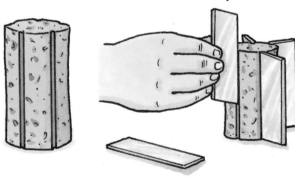

Ask an adult to cut slots into a cork.

Push the plastic strips into the cork.

Make 2 holes in the flower pot. Push the needles through these holes and into the cork.

Pour water over the blades of the wheel. Watch it spin.

24

It takes huge amounts of energy to heat and light our homes, offices and schools, to drive our cars and make all the things we use every day. But we need to be careful not to pollute our world and use up all the earth's resources.

Some problems seem so big that we may think there's nothing we can do about them.

LOOK BACK

Look back to pages 15, 22 and 23 to see how we can get the sun and wind to do our work for us.

But there is. You can help to save energy and reduce pollution by turning off lights when we do not need them. Re-use or recycle your waste – this saves using energy to make new things. Why not walk or go by bike rather than travel in a car?

More activities and facts

HAVE A GO!

Make a mini-greenhouse by cutting the bottom off a large plastic bottle. Put this over a patch of grass in your garden or at school. (You will need to lift the bottle every day to give this patch of grass some water.)

Check on the area every day for three or four weeks. Does the grass under the bottle look different from the grass around it? Note down what you see.

LOOK BACK

Look back to page 10 to find out about greenhouses. Ask your teacher why plants in greenhouses grow well if they are looked after properly.

FASCINATING FACT!

Recycling saves energy. We can recycle paper and cardboard, aluminium, glass and many different fabrics and clothes. Why not sort through the clothes you have grown out of and give them to some one else?

HAVE A GO!

You can have a go to see how insulation works (page 16). If you put on a vest, a t-shirt, a sweatshirt and a coat, air will get trapped between all these different layers. This stops the heat from your body escaping and so you keep warm.

 # LOOK BACK

Look back to page 13 to find out about energy from batteries. Some chemicals in batteries are poisonous. When they are dead, phone your local council to find out how to throw them away safely.

FASCINATING FACT!

Cars with their air conditioning systems on use up more fuel than cars with air conditioners turned off.

 # HAVE A GO!

Plants use light energy from the sun to make their food. This is called photosynthesis. Grow two lots of cress seeds on some damp cotton wool.

Put one lot in a sunny place . . .

. . . and the other in a dark cupboard. Which grows best?

Useful words

atmosphere: a layer of different gases that surrounds the earth.

acid rain: rainfall that absorbs the pollution from burning fuels like oil and coal. Acid rain can damage wildlife and buildings.

atom: a very tiny part of a chemical.

battery: a container which stores chemicals that mix together to make electricity.

carbon dioxide: a gas that is in the air. Carbon dioxide adds to the greenhouse effect.

chemicals: chemicals can be liquids, powders or gases that are mixed together to make other liquids, powders, gases or solids. Chemicals are found in batteries.

energy: the power that makes people, animals or machines move or work.

fossil fuel: plants and animals which died millions of years ago, were buried and have turned into coal, oil and gas are fossil fuels.

fuel: coal, gas and oil are types of fuel. They are burned to give us energy.

greenhouse effect: the warming up of the earth caused by greenhouse gases such as carbon dioxide.

insulation: materials that are used to keep things warm or cool.

pollute: to make the land, air or water dirty.

rechargeable: when a battery can be given more energy and used again, instead of having to be thrown away.

release: to let something go or to give out something. When fuels are burned, they release, or give out, energy.

resource: a stock or a supply of a material, such as coal or wood.

rot: when living things like plants and animals die and break down or decay.

solar energy: energy from the sun.

source: where something comes from.

Index

A

acid rain 10
atoms 8, 9

B

battery 13, 27
    rechargeable 13

C

carbon dioxide 11, 18
chemicals 8, 13, 27

E

electricity 9, 12, 13, 14, 22, 23, 24
energy 6, 7, 8, 9, 10, 12, 13, 14, 15, 16, 18, 19, 22, 24, 25, 27

F

fossil fuel 9, 10

fuel 6, 8, 9, 10, 11, 18, 21, 27
    burning of 10, 11, 18

G

greenhouse effect 10, 11, 26

I

insulation 16, 17, 27

P

pollute 10, 11, 18, 20, 25

R

recycle 19, 25, 26
resources 25
re-use 19, 25
rot 8

S

sources of energy 22, 24